THE THINGS GOD MADE

Explore God's Creation through the Bible, Science, and Art

ZONDERKIDZ

The Things God Made
Copyright © 2023 by Andy McGuire

Requests for information
should be addressed to:

Zonderkidz, 3900 Sparks Dr. SE,
Grand Rapids, Michigan 49546

ISBN 978-0-310-77127-2 (hardcover)
ISBN 978-0-310-77130-2 (ebook)

Editor: Katherine Jacobs
Design: Cindy Davis

Printed in Korea

23 24 25 26 27 28 /SAM/ 20 19 18 17 16 15 14 13 12 11 10 9 8 7 6 5 4 3 2 1

THE THINGS GOD MADE

Explore God's Creation through the Bible, Science, and Art

Andy McGuire

A long time ago, there was nothing but God.

He had an idea. He wanted there to be other things
besides just himself. So all of a sudden, out of nowhere and nothing ...

OM!

God made *everything*.

It didn't look like much at first. You wouldn't have recognized it. It was just a shapeless blob of matter and energy, like a lump of clay that hasn't been turned into something awesome yet.

But you wouldn't have been able to
see it anyway. It was dark everywhere.

So God said, "Let's have some light!"

And just like that, it happened.
Light everywhere.

But what, exactly, is light?

Light is what gives energy to the whole world. Plants use the power of light to live and grow. Then animals eat the plants so *they* can live and grow. And then we eat the plants and animals! In other words, we wouldn't be alive without light.

That's a hard question to answer. Light is mysterious. But here are some things we know about this mysterious and amazing creation called light. Even though we can see light, it is not quite a liquid, solid, or gas like other things God made. Sometimes it acts like a solid, but other times it acts more like energy—like a wave of water that splashes on the beach. When those waves of light hit our eyes, we see the light. And that light is made of all the colors of the rainbow! When we see all those colors of light at the same time, it looks white to our eyes.

And one more thing—light is superfast. There's nothing faster anywhere!

God looked around at what he'd made and liked what he saw.

God decided to organize what he'd made so far. He gathered up water in some places and land in other places.

How did God separate land from water? We can't be sure, but there are some clues in nature.

Hawaii used to be underwater too, but it appeared above the water in a different way. Melted rock from the center of the earth oozed out of cracks and holes that were on the outside of the earth. (It was like the jelly that leaks out of a donut when you bite into it.) As the melted rock cooled, it hardened and made huge mountains of land called volcanoes. A lot of the islands in the ocean were made this way.

Some parts of the world used to be completely underwater. Little by little the water got lower and lower in some of those places until land appeared.

Picture yourself in a bathtub with your knees completely covered by water. If you let some of the water go down the drain, you soon see your knees. That's what happened to places like Texas, Kansas, Australia, and the Sahara Desert. As the water went down, land appeared.

God looked at the land and water and liked what he saw.

God didn't want to leave the new ground bare. He made plants grow out of the soil that covered the ground. Plants begin as seeds and use water to grab very tiny bits of matter called nitrogen, phosphorus, and potassium out of the soil. These tiny bits are good plant food and help plants grow.

The plants God made were beautiful. He filled the land with pine trees and fruit trees, grasses and bushes. Some of the plants had beautiful flowers, and some of the trees had leaves that changed colors as the seasons changed.

Most plants are green, and there's a good reason for that. Plant leaves have something inside them called chlorophyll. You might remember that light is made up of all the colors of the rainbow. Chlorophyll absorbs light that gives energy to the plant. But chlorophyll ignores the green part of light because it isn't very good at turning air and water into food for them. Since the chlorophyll doesn't use the green part of light, the green light bounces back to our eyes—that's why leaves look green.

God made some unusual plants—plants of all shapes and sizes that grow in different parts of the world. He made rolling tumbleweeds that thrive in deserts, flat lily pads that float on ponds, and long vines that twist up tree trunks. He made each one in a special way so that it spreads its seeds to grow new plants in other places.

Plants live almost everywhere on earth. Seaweed and sea grasses grow in the ocean. A plant called algae grows on rocks. And cactuses grow in deserts.

Deserts are very dry, and cactuses have special features to help them live there. Their hard spines, which are a special kind of leaf, hold water much better than regular leaves do, and their shiny skin reflects the sunlight so they don't get too hot.

God looked at all the amazing plants and liked what he saw.

Next, God filled the sky with amazing and beautiful things! He made millions of galaxies filled with billions of stars and planets. Moons and comets swung through the air, flying around in perfect spins and twirls like a high-speed dance.

If you watch very carefully, you can use the stars and moon to mark off days, months, seasons, and holidays. For example, the moon slowly changes shape from full to completely dark and then back to full again, once a month. And you can see the planet Mars in the evening for most of the year. But during the last two months of the year, you can only see it in the morning.

The moon is beautiful, but it's more than just a decoration in the sky. The moon pulls on the earth like a magnet, which helps it stay balanced. That balance keeps our weather steady. If our weather changed too much, it would be hard for things to live on earth. Also, the moon slows down the earth's spinning. Without the moon, days would be less than ten hours long and the wind would be much too strong!

When this work was done, God looked up at the sky and liked what he saw.

Then God turned his attention to the water. He filled rivers and lakes with catfish and bass, walleye and trout, as well as non-fishy things like snails, river turtles, and crawdads.

And what magnificent creatures God made for the oceans! God created fearsome sharks, wiggly octopuses, and giant whales. He made spiky blowfish, pointy swordfish, and see-through jellyfish.

One tiny but very important sea creature is called coral. It looks like a wiggly little plant that attaches to the rocks on the floor of the ocean

Different animals in the ocean survive in different ways. Whales and dolphins are mammals, so they need to come up above the water to breathe air and get oxygen in their bodies. Fish, on the other hand, get oxygen out of the water that they take in through gills on the sides of their bodies.

The blue whale, the biggest whale of all, can be as long as two school buses end to end. While some fish, like sharks, eat other fish, the blue whale is enormous even though it only eats plankton, which are very tiny.

But coral is really tiny creatures that live off other teeny-tiny creatures in the water around it. (This actually helps to keep the surrounding waters clean and clear!) Millions of coral live together to build huge, colorful, underwater worlds for other creatures to live in, called reefs. Clown fish, eels, seahorses, and many other kinds of fish live there.

The ocean is a huge place. It covers seventy percent of the world's surface and in the deepest part it's almost seven miles down. That means, if Mount Everest, the tallest mountain in the world, was underwater in that deepest spot of the ocean, it would be covered by a mile of water!

Down near the ocean floor, there are fish that light up like tiny lamps. Animals like that are called "bioluminescent," which means living lights. Do you know any bioluminescent animals that might live near you? Hint: They fly through fields in the summertime, blinking on and off.

We don't know everything that lives at the bottom of the ocean. We know about some deep-sea creatures, like colossal squid, anglerfish, and giant spider crabs. But only God knows all the things that swim down there.

God looked into the water and liked what he saw.

The air needed animals too. God made birds to fly through the sky—graceful eagles, quiet owls, and beautiful parrots. There were also smart crows, colorful kingfishers, and silly ducks.

fast-moving air = low pressure

slower air = high pressure

Bird wings have a very special shape to help them fly. They are curved so the air on top of the wing goes faster than the air under the wing. Faster air is thinner and lighter than slower air. Because it's heavier, the air under the wing pushes harder on the wing than the lighter, faster air on top. Since the heavy air is pushing up from the bottom, it makes the bird go up—that's flying.

Many birds migrate, which means every year when the weather changes they fly somewhere else looking for food and safe nesting locations. Some birds, such as Canada geese, fly together for long distances in the shape of a V. Each goose takes a turn in front, facing the strongest wind, making it easier for the geese behind him so that not one goose gets too tired.

God made other flying creatures besides birds. Beautiful butterflies and enormous moths, bees and ladybugs and dragonflies—they all serve a purpose, doing exactly what God created them to do. For example, bees fly through fields looking for flowers filled with tasty nectar. The bees need the flowers, but the flowers need the bees too. The bees spread something called pollen from flower to flower, which helps the flowers make seeds that grow into new plants. That's why bees are fuzzy—the pollen sticks to the bee's fuzzy surface when it lands on a flower, and then it comes off when the bee rubs against another flower.

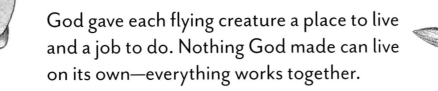

God gave each flying creature a place to live and a job to do. Nothing God made can live on its own—everything works together.

God looked at the sky and the creatures flying through it. He liked what he saw.

Birds need plants. Some parts they need to build their nests. And birds eat plant seeds. When birds eat them, they poop out some of the seeds, scattering them far and wide as they fly to distant lands. This helps plants spread to new places all around the world—part of God's plan.

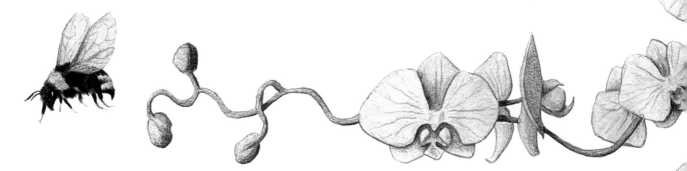

Cows and cow-like animals, such as bison and yaks, have unique stomachs so they can eat grass. Grass isn't good for people, but cow stomachs have four separate compartments to help them grind it up and break it down so that it's good for their bodies.

At last, it was time to fill the land with animals. God made spectacular creatures of all shapes and sizes—tall giraffes and silly apes, lazy sloths and scary crocodiles. Each one is unique and special, but they also have many things in common. All animals eat, breathe, move, and have babies that grow up to look like themselves. And animals have many of the same parts, like stomachs for eating and lungs for breathing.

All animals eat food, but they eat many different things. Foods that would be terrible for one creature are great for another. For example, beavers and termites eat wood—imagine that!

God gave each animal a different job to do. Beavers build dams, making ponds and swamps for themselves that other animals get to use and enjoy as well. Bees make honey that bears and badgers like to eat.

Animals, such as earthworms and prairie dogs, loosen up the ground to make it easier for seeds to grow.

Elephants who live in dry parts of Africa dig holes with their tusks and legs to findwater deep down in the ground. They maketheir own ponds! But the elephants don'tdo this just for themselves—other animals come from all over to enjoy a refreshing drink!

What fun God had filling up all the places he'd made: the deep, dark forests, the steep mountains, and the rolling, grass-covered prairies. He made graceful deer and horses, small, cuddly rabbits and chipmunks, and strong tigers and Komodo dragons.

God gave each of them what they needed to thrive wherever he put them. Tree-swinging monkeys have tails to grip a branch or a vine. Smooth-skinned lizards soak up energy from the sun in their desert homes. Furry polar bears stay cozy in the snow and ice up north.

Some animals that are "cousins" look very different depending on where they live. For example, jaguars are perfect for the rainforest, with their black spots on golden fur, blending into all the leafy shadows. Another animal in the cat family, snow leopards, have thick white and gray fur, which keeps them warm in the mountains and blends into the rocks and snow. They also have longer tails to help them balance as they climb steep mountainsides.

God looked around at all the animals he'd made and liked what he saw.

What was missing? God wanted creatures he could love as his very own children. They needed to think and talk and look like him.

So God made people—a man and a woman. They were smart and beautiful, made in God's own image, and he breathed himself into them. They were like him in very special ways.

God looked at everything he made …

One of the amazing ways people are like God is that we love to make things! Do you like to draw pictures? Sing songs? Write stories? Dance just for the fun of it? That's because God gave you a spark of creativity just like he has!

... and LOVED what he saw.

Find the small pictures that were in the boxes throughout the book,
such as the snow leopard, prairie dogs, geese, and bees.

Now, in the picture on the previous page, see if you can find:

- 6 bison
- 4 butterflies
- 1 jackrabbit
- 1 okapi (*You may have to look up what an okapi is!*)
- 2 wolves
- 1 lion
- 1 pine martin

- 3 kangaroos
- 2 armadillos
- 8 prairie dogs
- 1 hammerhead shark
- 3 swordfish
- 1 woodpecker

Author's Note

Pages 2–3: Genesis 1:1 "In the beginning, God created the heavens and the earth." There are several ways to interpret this verse. Is it kind of like a chapter heading, telling us what the next several verses will be about? Or is it saying that all at once, out of nothing, God made everything? Since verse 2 says that at first everything was formless and empty, I take it to mean that God started by making all the raw materials of the universe without it taking shape *just yet*. In other words, he created all the stuff that other stuff is made of, and *then* he formed it into something recognizable to us. This page boldly proclaims, "God made everything." On that I stand firm. When it comes to how he went about that, and what it looked like, I am much less certain. Throughout this book, I've tried to be faithful to Scripture and interpret it with humility. I ask for your grace if you read it or picture it differently.

Pages 4–5: Genesis 1:2 "Now the earth was formless and empty, darkness was over the surface of the deep, and the Spirit of God was hovering over the waters." This spread is a bit chaotic. Everything is without form. How does one draw something that is without form? This is my attempt.

Pages 6–7: Genesis 1:3 "And God said, 'Let there be light,' and there was light." Light is amazing, and if you haven't read about what light is, it's worth your time. I'd recommend a book called *Light* by Kimberly Arcand and Megan Watzke. It's a good read even if you don't like books on science.

Pages 8–9: Genesis 1:9 "And God said, 'Let the water under the sky be gathered to one place, and let dry ground appear.' And it was so." I love the idea of God gathering the waters, almost like a child uses his hands to shape sand on a beach. Did he do this supernaturally? Or did he use natural forces like volcanoes, earthquakes, and the evaporation of water into clouds (which, of course, are also made by God) to accomplish it? We don't know, but he certainly uses those things to continue to shape the earth today.

Pages 10–11: Genesis 1:11. "Then God said, 'Let the land produce vegetation: seed-bearing plants and trees on the land that bear fruit with seed in it, according to their various kinds.' And it was so." Notice that it's the land itself that produces the vegetation. What does that mean? I'm not sure, but it sounds like there were natural processes in play. This image is a grove of birches, one of my favorite trees—with their beautiful white bark. Birches grow quickly, but the wood is hard—harder than oak. The yellow flowers in the field and at the base of the closest tree are black-eyed Susans.

Pages 12–13: This page shows a variety of flowers, which are the seed-making parts of the plant. As you can see, they come in all sorts of shapes and colors, meant to attract bees and butterflies in order to spread their pollen far and wide (see page 24–25). Clockwise from the top left we have forget-me-nots, a ray flower, lily pads, a rose, and irises. Across the middle are twisting vines.

Pages 14–15: Genesis 1:14: "And God said, 'Let there be lights in the vault of the sky to separate the day from the night, and let them serve as signs to mark sacred times, and days and years.'" I've always been intrigued by the idea of the planets and stars serving to "mark sacred times." One example in Scripture is the magi following the star to Bethlehem. On this spread, Saturn is on the top left, with the Andromeda galaxy in the middle. Pluto is on the right, with Jupiter in the bottom right corner.

Pages 16–17: Genesis 1:20: "And God said, 'Let the water teem with living creatures.'" When I think of waters that "teem," coral reefs come to mind. What an incredibly varied and colorful ecosystem. Clockwise from the top left is a black-tipped reef shark, clown fish, green sea turtle, damselfish, and moray eel. On these pages are coral, which are made up of tiny animals. So I suppose, all told, there must be thousands of animals on this spread.

Pages 18–19: Genesis 1:21: "So God created the great creatures of the sea and every living thing with which the water teems and that moves about in it." In the ocean depths, strange creatures lurk. On the top left is a larval dendrochirus, with a small school of jellyfish swimming beside it. On the right side swim three silver spiny fish. At the bottom of the page an unknown creature yet to be discovered lies in wait for unsuspecting passersby.

Pages 20–21: Genesis 1:20: "And let birds fly above the earth across the vault of the sky." Flying is a mysterious phenomenon. While the explanation given here (called Bernoulli's theorem) is accurate, it only explains *some* of what enables flight. There are a lot of other factors involved, and even to this day there is disagreement among scientists about how exactly flight works. On the lefthand side of this spread is a greater bird-of-paradise. The other two birds are both Asian paradise flycatchers.

Pages 22–23: Genesis 1:22: "Be fruitful and increase in number and fill the water in the seas, and let the birds increase on the earth." Some translations talk about "winged creatures" rather than birds, so it's hard to be certain when non-bird flying creatures were created—butterflies, bees, moths, etc. They are certainly part of the fruitfulness of the earth, as they play a primary role in the reproduction of flowering plants. Clockwise from the top left is a damselfly, blue morpho butterfly, bumblebee, ladybug, atlas moth, scarab beetle, dragonfly, and hornet. The flowers, clockwise from the top left, are a cup-and-saucer vine, moth orchids, and tulips.

Pages 24–25: Genesis 1:24: "And God said, 'Let the land produce living creatures according to their kinds: the livestock, the creatures that move along the ground, and the wild animals, each according to its kind.'" The idea of the land itself "producing" living creatures is interesting to me. What, exactly, does the Scripture mean? One way of looking at it is that animals are made out of plants (it's what they eat to grow), and plants are made of dirt (it's where they get their nutrients). So, in that way, the land itself is making animals. But again, that's just one way of looking at it. This scene is in Mongolia, in Asia, which has vast plains as well as mountains. The animals on the left side are goitered gazelle. On the right are Bactrian camels (two-humped) and at the bottom are wild yaks. Domesticated yaks are some of the most productive animals of this region, providing milk, meat, and leather.

Pages 26–27: Elephants, like all creatures, are amazing in so many ways. This is an African savanna elephant. Despite our familiarity with elephants (we've domesticated Asian elephants for many, many centuries), it was only recently discovered that there are three species of elephant, not two. When I was in school, I learned the differences between Asian and African elephants, but as it turns out, there are two different species of African elephant—the savanna elephant and the forest elephant. Forest elephants eat mostly fruit, especially from large trees. They play a big role in dispersing seeds of these trees through the forest.

Pages 28–29: The remarkable adaptability of animals is on full display in wintry climates like Siberia, depicted on this spread. That creatures can survive in places with temperatures that vary by over 100 degrees is truly remarkable to me. I live in Minnesota, where it can be over 100 degrees Fahrenheit in the summer and 20 below in the winter. And yet I see deer, squirrels, and coyotes all year round. On the top left is a Siberian roe deer, looking nervously at the Amur tiger (sometimes called a Siberian tiger) on the right. There are several red squirrels hiding here and there. Squirrels are so common I sometimes forget how remarkable they are. They are one of the most adaptable animals on the planet (and if you've ever tried to keep them out of your birdfeeder you know how wily they can be).

Pages 30–31: Genesis 1:26: "Then God said, 'Let us make mankind in our image, in our likeness.'" All of us, old and young, male and female, every race and tribe, are created in God's very image. It's hard to fathom what that really means, but at the very least we know it means he cares deeply for each and every one of us. Of course no one knows what Adam and Eve looked like, but I have given them skin color and features that defy easy categorization. Somehow Adam and Eve contained all the DNA of the human race, and they and their children were truly fruitful, spreading humanity to every corner of the globe.

Bibliography

"African Forest Elephant," https://www.worldwildlife.org/species/african-forest-elephant.

American Museum of Natural History. *Ocean: The Definitive Visual Guide*. 2014, Dorling Kindersley Limited. Pages 170, 260–272.

Anderson, Miles. *Cacti & Succulents*. 2008, Anness Publishing Ltd. Pages 8–13.

Arcand, Kimberly and Watzke, Megan. *Light: The Visible Spectrum and Beyond*. 2015, Black Dog and Leventhal Publishers. Pages 9–16.

Breithaupt, Jim. *Physics: A Complete Introduction*. 2019, John Murray Press. Pages 121–184.

Eason, Sarah. *How Does a Jet Plane Work?* 2010, Gareth Stevens Publishing. Page 8.

https://www.insidescience.org/video/what-would-happen-if-there-were-no-moon. Accessed on 6/11/21.

Laidlaw, Rob. *5 Elephants*. 2014, Fitzhenry & Whiteside. Page 14.

https://lostinaustralia.org/australia-mystery-inland-ocean. Accessed on 7/19/21.

https://nineplanets.org/questions/what-would-happen-if-there-was-no-moon/. Accessed on 6/11/21.

https://www.quantamagazine.org/why-are-plants-green-to-reduce-the-noise-in-photosynthesis-20200730/. Accessed on 7/19/21.

Smithsonian Knowledge Encyclopedia. 2013, Dorling Kindersley Limited. Pages 88–91.

https://www.theguardian.com/science/2019/jul/12/sahara-was-home-to-some-of-largest-sea-creatures-study-finds. Accessed on 7/19/21.